Greetings fr OLD SALFOR

A PICTORIAL JOURNEY THROUGH OLD SALFORD'S PAST

Edward Gray

A Memories publication

in association with the

© Published by:

in association with

Manchester EveningNews

Memories,
222 Kings Road,
Firswood,
Manchester M16 OJW,
Tel: 0161 862 9399

Reprint organised by

_liff Hayes

ISBN - 1 899181 13 X

ACKNOWLEDGEMENTS

The author records his thanks to Tim Ashworth and Tony Frankland, of the Salford Local History Library, for their unfailingly cheerful assistance in seeking out the answers to many queries; to Andrew Cross, Salford City Archivist, for making available past records; and to fellow-collectors Mark A.I. Fynn and Stephen Walker.

Printed and bound by: **MFP Design & Print**.
Longford Trading Estate, Thomas Street,
Stretford, Manchester, M32 OJT.
Tel: 0161 864 4540.

FOREWORD

The producers of the first picture postcards unknowingly provided a fascinating history of life as it was early in the twentieth century. The views captured through the lenses of their cameras some 70 or 80 years ago enable us to consider some places which have changed a little, and others which have changed a great deal — not always for the better. To the casual browser amongst these pages, it may seem that in those far off days the sun shone all the time and it never rained, but there are a couple of snow scenes included, to prove that the early photographers were hardy souls, who, on some occasions at least, braved unsuitable weather conditions with their cumbersome equipment in order to record the local scene.

The illustrations come from the author's collection of old picture postcards of the area. It was not easy to decide which cards to include or exclude, but the selection has been made in an attempt to avoid using views which are well-known, or which have been used elsewhere in other publications. Thus, some famous landmarks, such as the Walkden Memorial, have been omitted in favour of less-common scenes.

The 'Golden Age' of the picture postcard is considered to be the years 1900-1918, with sales at a peak about 1905. The main reason for the popularity of the postcard was that it could be sent for only one halfpenny, whilst the normal letter rate was double this figure at one whole penny. Plain postcards had been permitted by the Post Office as early as 1870, offering one side for the address only, and the other for a message. In 1902, however, a revision of the regulations allowed one side to be divided, half the space being for a brief message and the other half for the address. This so-called 'divided back' gave the chance to use the whole of the front of the card for an illustration or advertisement, and the artists and photographers of the Edwardian period were not slow to seize their opportunity.

Local and national photographers recorded the changing scenes and events at the beginning of the century, and new printing techniques were employed to produce high-quality picture postcards. The cards, priced one penny or less, were often purchased for their own sake, and many remained unposted, finding their way into the family album. A collecting craze ensued, and collectors regularly exchanged cards through the post — ''Another one for your album'' is a familiar and frequent message. People sent cards to show relatives and friends where they lived, and many were used as birthday or Christmas greetings cards. Whilst national firms, such as Valentine's or Frith's, would record the main streets and buildings, and print such cards by the hundreds, local publishers would photograph the smaller side-streets, even individual houses, for which the potential sales figures would be very low.

The boom years for the picture postcard trade ended in 1918, when the postage rate was doubled. Far fewer local picture postcards were produced in the 1920s, and thereafter only the most common city centre views and the seaside comic cards were easily available.

Amongst the local postcard publishers from the early years of the century were W. Whittaker & Company of Irlams O' Th' Height, who survived the collapse of the trade by becoming paper bag merchants; Charles Wilkinson, who became a wholesale stationer; William Boden, a chemist of Worsley Road, Winton, who published postcards as a side-line to his main business until 1912; Charles Downs of Trafford Road, who specialised in ship photography in Salford Docks; and Horatio (Harry) Grundy, of Eccles, who persevered in the postcard trade into the 1920s, and who was to be seen calling upon newsagents and stationers, carrying an attache case full of his latest prints of the area, which he hoped would be stocked by the shopkeepers. Those early photographers could never have imagined the value which is placed on their work today. To them, and to other unknown photographers, the local historian of today is indebted for a unique social record of the period.

Readers should perhaps be reminded that Salford, as we know it today, has grown through boundary extensions, firstly in 1853, when it absorbed the former separate townships of Pendleton and Broughton, and secondly in 1974, when the reoganisation of local government absorbed Eccles, Irlam, Swinton & Pendlebury and Worsley. All these districts are represented by illustrations in this book. Prices are given in pre-decimal coinage, when there were 240 pennies, or 20 shillings, to the pound.

Some of the main changes in the local scene have resulted from housing or other improvements, but many are a consequence of the rise in popularity of the private motor car, which has led to a corresponding reduction in the provision of public transport services during the last 30 years or so. Many railway stations, even whole lines, have closed; the municipal bus undertaking vanished in 1969; and the subsequent services of the Greater Manchester Passenger Transport Authority have diminished. The city we once knew has been sliced into sections by motorways, or other road schemes, designed by the urban planners to allow motorists to pass through Salford with the greatest possible speed. In these alterations, a great deal of value has been swept away irrevocably. Not all change is bad, of course, but there is no doubt that some of the postcards reproduced in this book will evoke feelings of nostalgia for an era which has now gone for ever.

Edward Gray.
Salford, 1991.

Ted Gray.

Dedicated to my wife Kathleen,
who encouraged me to compile this book.

The multi-view postcard was popular for posting to friends who wished to learn something of the sender's home town. This sort of card was usually made up from four or five views, all of which would be available as separate postcards in their own right, but which had been cut and mounted with appropriate art-work, to be re-photographed to produce a new negative from which to make the composite print. This particular example, posted to an address in Dublin in March 1905, offered good value for the penny it probably cost, since it included no fewer than thirteen views. The sender refers to the extended tennis courts in Buile Hill Park, which, she writes, "should be ready for Whit Week." This may explain the choice of card, since a section of the courts is included centre right. Other locations featured include Peel Park; the Technical School; Seedley Park; the Drill Hall on Cross Lane; Broad Street; and the Nurses' Home on The Crescent. The card does not carry any publisher's imprint, but the probability is that it was *not* a local firm, for the view chosen for the central top position, shows Trafford Park boating lake, and Trafford Park was not, and still is not, part of Salford. The Salford Extension Act of 1853 incorporated the former separate townships of Broughton and Pendleton, and local government reorganisation of 1974 drew in Eccles, Irlam, Swinton & Pendlebury, and Worsley, but Trafford Park remains firmly over the border.

Salford.

Chapel Street.

Building of the original Salford Town Hall was begun in 1825, when the foundation stone was laid by Lord Bexley, Chancellor of the Duchy of Lancaster, after whom the square is named. This view shows the Town Hall and Bexley Square in 1903. The small building in the middle of the square was a cabmen's shelter, long since gone, which reflected the profusion of horse-drawn transport which was common in the Edwardian period. One hansom cab appears on the left. The corner shop occupied by D. Williams, Meat Purveyor, was in later years replaced by the Electricity Board building, but the Town Hall itself and some of the buildings in the square remain.

Another view of Chapel Street, looking towards The Crescent, shows (on the left) the branch of the Manchester & Liverpool District Bank on the corner of Irwell Street, whilst buildings on the right, beyond Bexley Square, include the Church Inn at the corner of Ford Street, the Salford Education Offices (new in 1895, and still existing), and Salford Cathedral. The ornate poles, with their fancy wrought-iron scroll work, were placed in the middle of the road to support the overhead wires for the electric tramway system, inaugurated in 1901. On the top of the poles may be noted the new electric lamps for the street lighting, though the older gas lamps remain on the pavements.

THE KING UNVEILING FUSILIERS MEMORIAL

On the 13th July 1905 King Edward VII and Queen Alexandra visited the city for the purpose of opening a new dock. The royal couple were staying with Lord Derby at Knowsley Hall, and on their way from the Docks to return to their train at Victoria Station, they paused first to receive civic officials in Peel Park, and then to unveil the Memorial Statue to the Lancashire Fusiliers, sited at the end of Oldfield Road opposite to Salford Royal Hospital. Stands had been provided for onlookers along the route of the royal procession, and the visit was recorded by many postcard photographers. This example, taken from a point in front of the hospital, and looking down Oldfield Road, reveals that a long cord had been provided from the covering flag, so that the King did not need to dismount from his carriage to perform the unveiling ceremony. Beyond the statue, slightly to the right in the upper portion of the picture, may be noted the end of the Oldfield Road 'Dwellings,' a gloomy block of tenements, originally constructed by the London & North Western Railway Company to house their servants. The Fusiliers' Memorial has recently (1991) been re-sited a few yards away from its original location to permit alterations at the junction.

A later postcard of the same spot at the corner of Oldfield Road and Chapel Street, but looking in the opposite direction, shows the 1911 extensions to Salford Royal Hospital. The patch of new brickwork on the left betrays the original site of the main entrance portico, whose impressive columns, with coat-of-arms above, were moved to their new location in the centre of the picture during the rebuilding. The rear of the Fusiliers' statue may be seen in front of that entrance. The First World War tank and field gun (centre left) were placed on display at this spot, and remained there for many years.

Some local postcard photographers would offer to take pictures such as this shop front, with the proprietor and family included, hoping that an order for several prints would result, and that the owner might use the card for advertising his business. Such cards are often of interest for the range of wares and the prices displayed. This example shows the shop of Samuel Livesley, wholesale and retail grocer and provision dealer, of 22 Oldfield Road, Salford, where the proprietor traded for 55 years up to his death in 1938. The lady is, presumably, his wife, Hannah Mary, and his daughter stands atop a large Jacob's biscuit box. Note the advertisements for Oxo, Bovril and the now unknown 'Ju-Vis' beef tea, priced at 2 ounces for 6½d or 4 ounces for 11½d.

Another shop-front postcard shows the premises of the appropriately-named Albert Edward Baker, at 86 Regent Road, Salford, about 1911-12. The longitudonal sign above the name announces that Mr. Baker trades "also at 20 Eccles New Road and 527-529 Eccles New Road, Weaste." The sign in the window above the lady's head informs customers that Crawford's Butter Puffs, at 7d per pound, are "delightful with preserves, stewed fruits, or cheese," whilst the window posters read "Try our splendid bread. It is sure to please."

The triangle at the Broad Street end of Cross Lane, viewed here from Windsor Bridge, was always an important junction. This postcard, sent to Cardiff in 1904, shows the then new Salford Royal Hippodrome, which opened for business in March 1904. The theatre held two performances nightly, at 7.00 and 9.00 p.m., with seat prices at twopence, fourpence, sixpence and one shilling. The Grapes Hotel is to the left of the theatre, and centre right is the tramway waiting room and toilets, from behind which may be seen part of the obelisk, erected in 1893 in memory of Oliver Heywood, a local philanthropist. Hidden from view, but lying between the Hippodrome and Broad Street, was the large house, set back from the road, which for many years was the home of Hall's Herbal Remedies. The open-top tramcar is turning from Windsor Bridge into Cross Lane, whilst the group of small boys and youths are showing a keen interest in the photographer and his equipment. The Salford Hippodrome, later re-named the Windsor Theatre, closed in 1956, and nothing now remains of this scene except for the obelisk, which survives in the middle of a new McDonald's Restaurant development.

Cross Lane was the site of an important cattle market, founded as early as 1774. Cattle and sheep pens extended for a considerable distance from Cross Lane between Unwin Street and West High Street, where there was also an abattoir. The building in the centre of the view, sporting a clock tower, was occupied by two banks, Parr's Bank to the left, the Union Bank to the right. Herds of animals often arrived via the railway cattle sidings in Liverpool Street, and were driven along Cross Lane to the market. In later years, the site became the venue for the Whitsun and Christmas visits of the travelling fairground, and then was developed as a mixed retail market. The area is now occupied by the civic housing estate and Windsor High School off Churchill Way.

REGENT THEATRE, SALFORD.

Cross Lane was famous for its large number of public houses, but it also boasted a theatre at each end. Close to its junction with Regent Road was the Regent Theatre, later renamed the Palace Theatre, which, 1929-1956, became mainly a cinema. In fact, the building contained *two* large halls, because to the right of the theatre's auditorium was the Regent Assembly Rooms, entered by the far side. On the left of the picture is the Ship Hotel, on the corner of Eccles New Road, owned by Walker & Homfray's Salford Brewery. Notice the young tramway employee (who appears to have three legs), stationed with iron in hand, to change the points for the electric tramcars at this major junction. His shelter in inclement weather was the hut by the tram stop on the right. The photograph was taken about 1912.

People who use the roundabout at the end of the M602 with its car showrooms and single church spire should study this next picture carefully. This was once the scene at that spot. A few yards across the junction from the previous picture was Trafford Road, seen here in a 1914 view. Again, the Ship Hotel and the Palace Theatre may be noted in the centre, together with a distant view of the tower of Cross Lane barracks. On the left is Stowell Memorial Church, dating from 1869. The sender of the card, in addition to the message on the back, has written in the left corner 'You can see our house from this church.' At the side of the church, horse-drawn cabs from the 'Trafford Road Stand' await clients. The old underground conveniences and the Police Box (often in use during riotous nights at the 'Ship') occupy the corner of Eccles New Road. The poles in the centre of the road, which once supported the overhead wires, have been replaced by side-poles as a consequence of increased road traffic. Regent Road to the right of the junction was once a lively and prosperous shopping area, the whole of which has now been destroyed in favour of road 'improvements.' Stowell's spire, but not the church itself, has been retained as a landmark. At this crossroads the tramway junction, one of the largest in the British Isles, and known as a 'grand union' (in that it had two lines around each of the four corners and two across in every direction), remained buried under post-war road surfacing, but during the motorway construction work, the opportunity was taken to lift the trackwork in sections. It has been taken to Crich, Derbyshire, the home of the National Tramway Museum, where it is hoped one day to re-assemble the complete junction for display purposes.

The southern stretch of Trafford Road increased in importance after the opening of the Manchester Ship Canal in 1894. New buildings reflected the activities of the docks alongside. In this view, posted in 1910, the Custom House, at present a Grade 2 listed building, but threatened by a road-widening scheme, appears in the right foreground. It remained in use by H.M.Customs until the opening of a new Customs House on the Dock Estate in 1970. Since then, it has served a variety of uses, but has been allowed to deteriorate. In the centre of the view, the building flying the large flag, was the 'Flying Angel' Mission to Seamen, and beyond it the Salisbury Hotel. The Hotel was owned by Groves & Whitnall, another Salford brewery, based on Regent Road. It was a superior hotel for the area, and boasted a fine dining room and good residential accommodation. A well-remembered feature was the collection of large ship models displayed in glass cases on the staircase. Beyond the Salisbury buildings, on the extreme left of the view can be seen the entrance to Ordsall Park. Comparison with illustration number 3, will reveal that the Trafford Road residents had not yet been favoured with electric street lamps on top of the tramway poles. The district is now altered almost beyond recognition by the Salford Quays development.

A feature of the terraced streets in the old Ordsall area of Salford was the ubiquitous 'corner shop,' which usually functioned as an 'off-licence' and general store. This example shows a Groves & Whitnall outlet, situated at 106 Derby Street, at the corner of New Cambridge Street, Ordsall, managed by Charles W. Thornton, "licenced to sell by retail beer to be consumed off the premises," Mr. Thornton himself, standing in the doorway with his wife, was the writer of this postcard, sent to his mother in Barnsley in 1909.

TRAFFORD ROAD BRIDGE

At the boundary with Stretford, the course of the Irwell had been deepened and straightened in the construction of the Manchester Ship Canal, and although the main terminal docks lay in Salford, four smaller docks for coastal shipping lay on the Manchester side of the waterway on the site of what had been Pomona Gardens. At Trafford Road, as at other places on the canal, bridges had to be capable of swinging in order to permit the passage of large ships. In this 1903 view of Trafford Bridge, taken from the Stretford side, the fixed bridge over the original watercourse may be seen in the middle distance, with the new swing bridge, complete with flock of sheep, one cow, and a pony and trap, in the foreground. The chimney and boiler house for the hydraulic operation of the bridge are centre left, with the control cabin partly hidden from view. On the edge of the picture can be seen part of a Manchester tramcar, whilst on the other side of the bridge, Salford tramcars reverse in Trafford Road. It may be noted that the tramlines do not yet cross the bridge. The Ship Canal Engineer was left to solve the difficult problem of exact alignment of both lines and overhead wires before tramcars were able to cross in 1905.

A 1906 postcard shows the bridge in the process of turning. Gates were swung into position across the roadway before the bridge opened, and spectators would crowd to watch the ship pass. When the bridge was swinging back into position, the bridgemen always opened the right-hand gates first, allowing pedestrians to cross before the vehicles, and small boys often had the pleasure of stepping onto the moving bridge to enjoy the last few inches of motion. In later years, long queues of road vehicles would build up, and it was particularly irksome to find the bridge swinging in the 'rush hour' period for Trafford Park workers. The problem of overhead wires had been solved. Note the new gantry and centre pole, not present on the earlier picture. Comparison with the previous picture will also reveal that what appears to be a globe (actually a basketwork sphere) on a pole on the top of the bridge has changed position. In the days before radio communication, the basket was raised or lowered as a signal to ship's masters, indicating who had right of way in approaching the bridge. Although in daylight the ship's crew would be able to see whether or not the bridge was open or closed, if the bridge lay on a bend (as at Trafford Bridge) the crew might not see a vessel approaching in the opposite direction, with the consequent danger of a collision at the narrow point. When the basket was down, it meant 'Do not approach'; when fully raised, 'The inward-bound vessel may proceed.' During darkness, coloured lights were used. The lone basket was soon joined by a smaller one, placed immediately underneath, in order to remove any uncertainty — when the large top one alone was raised, the inward-bound vessel could proceed; when both were raised, the outward-bound vessel could proceed; when both were lowered, the bridge was closed to shipping. At the time of writing, the bridge has been repainted to advertise the smart Salford Quays development, but the two basket globes remain in position, unused and disregarded.

DELEMERE UNLOADING FRUIT &c.

Postcards of individual ships berthed in Salford Docks were produced and sold by Trafford Road newsagents for merchant seamen to send to their families. Views of vessels of the Prince Line, Manchester Liners, and other regular visitors were common. Charles Downs, a postcard publisher of Trafford Road, produced little else. However, photographs of the dock workers were rare, and this 1908 postcard by T. Pinder of Rochdale is one of only a few of this type. Whilst the men in the foreground enjoy a tea-break, others struggle with cases of fruit from the S.S. 'Delemere.' Quite who Mr.Pinder hoped would buy his postcard is not known, but the message on the back indicates that he must have had some success amongst the dockers. It was posted to a friend in Whitehaven by 'J.W.' who wrote, ''There are some faces on this card that you know.''

SALFORD DOCK MISSION BOY'S BRASS BAND.

The district of Ordsall, so much influenced by the proximity of the Docks and the industrial estate of Trafford Park, enjoyed a social and religious life of its own. One of the centres of leisure activities was the Dock Mission, and many postcards have survived showing the various dramatic, musical, educational, and social enterprises which the Mission's volunteer workers organised. Here is a postcard by Salford photographer J. Shorten, showing the members of the Dock Mission Boys' Brass Band, attired in their Sunday-best, all with clean white collars. Many people will remember the Dock Mission as being at the side of Ordsall Park, but, in fact, its first activities took place in a Mission Hall on Taylorson Street, next to St. Cyprian's Church. Later, about 1915, the Mission moved to take over the former Ordsall Park Wesleyan Chapel on New Park Road.

Manchester Racecourse, which, like Manchester Docks and Manchester Exchange Railway Station, was always in Salford, was located on the New Barns Estate, close to Trafford Road, lying between the River Irwell (later the Ship Canal) and Broadway. When the Ship Canal Company wished to construct a large new dock, negotiations were begun to purchase the New Barns land. This photograph of the racecourse, taken from the top of the grain elevator on Trafford Wharf, shows the course beyond the timber storage area, looking towards Howard Street and Eccles New Road (top left), where the spire of Stowell's Church may be noted. Trafford Road and Number 8 Dock are top right. Note the grandstands (upper centre left) on the edge of the course, and the rear of the old Trafford Road School (upper centre right). The last race meeting at New Barns was held in 1901, after which excavations began for the construction of the new Number 9 Dock.

The new dock was completed in 1905. Here is one of a series of postcards published to show stages in the construction work. The remains of one of the racecourse grandstands may be seen at the bottom of Howard Street, with Stowell's spire to the right. Contractors' materials obliterate much of the turf. The dock has not yet been filled with water, allowing the construction of the dock walls on piers to remain visible. The area is now part of the new Salford Quays development.

For the opening of the new Number 9 Dock, at three-quarters of a mile long the largest in the terminal complex, a temporary pavilion was erected for the occasion of the visit of King Edward VII and Queen Alexandra on the 13th July 1905. The new dock remained separated from the canal proper, but had been flooded to the correct level by allowing water to enter from the main canal by way of a small cut made in the retaining wall. This wall had been left in place between the new dock and the main waterway, but had been drilled and filled with a series of explosive charges, which the King was invited to detonate by operating the lever placed on the table before him. The resulting explosions were designed to collapse the wall, after which two Mersey ferry boats, the 'Bidston' and the 'Claughton,' hired for the occasion and laden with specially-invited guests, were to sail into the new dock and moor in front of the pavilion. The plan did not proceed without a slight hitch, however, for after the detonations part of the wall appeared to have remained in place, and there was a slight delay before it was deemed safe for the two boats to enter the dock. A local journalist, reporting the event, wrote. "The King appeared to be in good humour, and laughed heartily." Behind the pavilion, the King inspected several volunteer and cadet regiments from all parts of Lancashire, before proceeding to Peel Park, (see page 7). The royal visit was well-recorded by postcard photographers. This example was produced by Renaud, of Chorlton-cum-Hardy, and shows the King, in plumed hat, standing before the table, on which is the detonating lever and a sectional model of the planned warehousing construction. The remains of the retaining wall were later pulled from the canal bed by mechanical dredgers.

The first Manchester Races had been held on Kersal Moor, but from 1847 to 1867 the organisers leased the Castle Irwell estate of the Fitzgerald family, before purchasing a site at New Barns. However, with the proceeds of the New Barns sale to the Manchester Ship Canal Company, the racecourse committee purchased outright the whole of the Castle Irwell lands which lay within a meander of the River Irwell, close to the Broughton boundary, and in 1902 the Races returned to their former home. The main entrance gates and grandstands were constructed at the Cromwell Road end of the course. Racing continued here until the November Handicap of 1963, after which the main building (seen in this view) was utilised for a short while as a restaurant and hospitality suite. Land and buildings were eventually taken over for student accommodation for the University of Salford.

The stables of the Castle Irwell Racecourse were positioned at the end of the course furthest from the Cromwell Road entrance. In this view of Kersal and the River Irwell, taken by photographer Mr. Ward of Great Clowes Street, the stables and estate maintenance department may be seen centre left. The distant view includes some of the fine houses of Kersal, which enjoyed a fine prospect over the river, golf and race courses from the Bury New Road side of the meander. To the right of the picture, on the upper reaches of Lower Broughton Road at 'The Cliff,' occurred the 1927 landslip.

21

The early postcard photographers tended to concentrate on street scenes or posed groups of people. Interior views, probably because of lighting problems in the days before electronic flash, were comparatively rare. Here is an unusual view which the sender has noted as being the "laundry class at Grecian Street School". The school was built close to Albert Park and not far from the bridge in the previous view, in 1888. This photograph dates from about 1902. Note the mangle for wringing wet clothes, the small washing bowls, and the smoothing irons.

The River Irwell marked the boundary between the once-separate townships of Pendleton and Broughton. Cromwell Bridge, just beyond the Racecourse entrance, was constructed in 1882. This postcard, dating from about 1905, is taken looking towards Broughton along Great Cheetham Street. The large building on the right across the bridge is the Griffin Hotel, on the corner of Lower Broughton Road. This bridge was replaced by the present structure in 1934, when the opportunity was taken to double the tramway track, the last new length of line to be constructed in the city.

21801   BROUGHTON LANE. LOWER BROUGHTON.

Broughton Lane, Lower Broughton, a postcard in the 'Grosvenor Real Photograph Series,' dating from about 1907. The location is the junction of Broughton Lane and Camp Street, which lies to the left of the large street lamp. The impressive lamp carries the 'All Cars Stop Here' sign, 'cars' meaning tramcars at this period. Note also the horizontal bracket on which the gas lamp attendant could rest his ladder, a standard feature of such street fittings. The open-top tramcar, on its way to Deansgate via Great Clowes Street, is about to enter the single-track section on the narrower portion of the road, and the guard consequently keeps a careful watch on the trolley rope. Broughton Town Hall was situated in Duke Street, off Broughton Lane, and many civic officials were owners or tenants of the large houses nearby, within walking distance of their place of work. 'Tudor Villa,' at 178 Broughton Lane, was occupied by John Thomas Morris, described as 'The Collector of the District and Highway Rate,' with his office in Broughton Town Hall.

THE LAKE, ALBERT PARK, LOWER BROUGHTON. N.

In 1877 the civic authorities opened Albert Park, Lower Broughton, which quickly became a popular spot for local residents. It was well-photographed by postcard publishers, and a favourite view was of the lake and bridge, sometimes titled ''The Swans' Retreat.'' This card was posted in 1911 to a gentleman working for an English company in Lagos, Nigeria, to remind him how pleasant the summer was at home in Broughton.

Another favourite view of Albert Park was the long central walk, lined with classical statues, a much-frequented haunt on summer evenings. This view, looking towards Great Clowes Street, includes a gathering of local children, apparently in their best clothes, which indicates that the photograph was probably taken on a Sunday. Note the young boys on their tyre-less tricycles. Sadly, in the 1980s, officers of the then Recreational Services Department, guardians of the city's parks and gardens, destroyed forever a large portion of this pleasant and attractive amenity, and substituted in its stead a dreary expanse of featureless 'all-weather' floodlit sports pitches.

A mid-1920s postcard of Great Cheetham Street East, although titled "St.James's Church, Broughton," appears to have been taken as much to include the motor bus as the church. The location is at the junction with Leicester Road. The solid-tyred Leyland motor bus was new in 1923-24, and is seen in service on Salford's first bus route, between Broughton and Weaste. St.James's Church was consecrated in 1879.

This fine view of Bury New Road, Higher Broughton, looking towards Manchester, shows its junction with Great Clowes Street at The Cliff, scene of the disastrous landslip after a severe storm in 1927, which has closed that portion of the road to the right ever since. Bury New Road itself, remarkably free from traffic and therefore probably another Sunday picture, displays the ornate centre poles for the tramway overhead. The church on the left, at the corner of Northumberland Street, was the North Manchester New Jerusalem Church. A trio of children gazes with interest at the photographer, whilst the cyclist is careful to ride between, rather than on, the tramlines. Many a cyclist will remember the problems which ensued if a wheel became caught in the groove of the tram rail!

Bella Vista, the large house at the corner of Broom Lane and Bury New Road, Higher Broughton (to the left of the junction in the previous photograph) was for many years a private school, the Broughton & Crumpsall High School, Headmistress Miss E.M.Clarke. Later, taken over by the local education authority, and with appropriate extensions added in 1927, it was the Broughton High School For Girls. The photographer on this occasion managed to capture the workman upon his ladder evidently adjusting the cables for the tramway wires. Note the 'ALL CARS STOP HERE' sign attached to the pole, the workman's handcart, the ornate lamps, and what appears to be a signalling device with three lenses on the pole above the lamps.

KERSAL MOOR ROAD, HIGHER BROUGHTON.

This postcard is titled "Kersal Moor Road, Higher Broughton" although the road is better known as Moor Lane, and shows an easterly view up the slope towards Bury New Road. In the middle distance is St. Paul's Church, Kersal, consecrated in 1862, with its distinctive spires, and on the left the associated schools, where the Rev. Arthur Leathley, B.A. Oxon., was for many years the Principal. Kersal Moor itself lay to the north behind the schools. No traffic is visible, save for the horse-drawn cart making its way up the hill. The schools have gone, but the church remains.

KERSAL BAR, HR BROUGHTON.

The boundary between Broughton and Prestwich crossed Bury New Road just north of its junction with Moor Lane and Singleton Road. The junction became known as Kersal Bar because of the location of a toll bar on this former turnpike road connecting Bury and Manchester. In this view, taken about 1904, the house built for the tollbar keeper is on the left, serving as a base for a plumbing and cycle repair business. Until recently, the building remained in use as a general store, newsagent and stationer's shop, but at the time of writing (1991) the premises appear closed and neglected. This postcard is also one of the 'Grosvenor Series,' and was taken looking north towards Bury. This spot, Kersal Bar, was the Higher Broughton terminus of the region's first horse-drawn tramway in 1877, and was also the first out-of-town terminus for the new electric tramcars in 1901. By 1902-03 the electric tramway had been extended to serve Prestwich and Whitefield, from which direction the open-top tramcar has arrived on its way to Eccles via Manchester. Note the cabmen's shelter and cabs at the entrance to Moor Lane.

The former townships of Pendleton and Broughton, separated by the River Irwell, were incorporated with Salford in 1853. Pendleton extended from a point near the end of Cross Lane as far as Irlams O'Th'Height in one direction, and to the Eccles boundary in another. This 1904 view of Broad Street, Pendleton, looking in a north-westerly direction, shows how aptly named was the street. The young boy in the foreground was evidently unaware of the photographer — he has taken off his jacket, and presents only a back view of his braces — but the gentleman leaning on the lamp-post further along is eyeing the cameraman with hostile suspicion. Ornate tramway standards, bearing the new street lighting, occupy the centre of the roadway, but gas lamps remain on the sidewalks. To the right of the picture is the Brunswick Methodist Church, dating from 1881. The church itself has gone, but the adjoining schoolroom survived in use as an outpost of the College of Technology, and now accommodates offices and a nursery. The terraced buildings in the centre distance have also survived.

The focal point of Pendleton was considered to be St. Thomas's Church and the former Pendleton Town Hall at the junction of Broad Street and Broughton Road. Pendleton Town Hall was an impressive building, architecturally attractive, and had it survived a few years longer, it might well have become the subject of a preservation order. Unfortunately, it was demolished in the 1970s, and the site remains merely an undeveloped car park. St. Thomas's Church dates from 1831, and now stands alongside the traffic island above the A6 roadworks, the area to the right of the picture (formerly 'Hanky Park' in the old Hankinson Street area) having been developed with tower blocks of flats and the Salford Shopping Precinct. The width of the road permitting such an extravagance, the tramways here had a three-track layout to enable trams turning back at Pendleton to wait without obstructing other through services. This card was posted in 1905 to Fall River, Massachusetts, North America, with no message, addressed only to Master William Harley of 615 Middle Street. The sender could never have imagined that his postcard would return to its town of origin some 80 years later.

WOOLPACK INN, PENDLETON.

The site at the junction of Eccles Old Road and Bolton Road, Pendleton, had been occupied by an inn since at least 1814. It was also the location of the toll bars of the Pendleton Turnpike Trust until about 1870. The Woolpack Hotel, (a Walker & Homfray Hotel) at first did not have its mock half-timbered front. In front of the hotel were two drinking troughs for horses, a provision made at most junctions, and a drinking fountain, with chained metal cups, for humans. Many postcards of this spot were produced, some titled 'The Fountain, Pendleton,' others 'The Big Lamp.' The richly-decorated lamp was certainly big — it dwarfs the tramcars and carts in this picture from 1903. The Hotel was demolished in 1967 to make way for road improvements, which seem designed mainly to allow motorists to pass through Salford more speedily.

Eccles Old Road was a leafy thoroughfare which attracted many of the rich Manchester merchants to move out of the city centre in the nineteenth century, and to set up large homes along its length. It remains one of the most pleasant main roads in the city. This photograph, looking towards Eccles, was taken near the junction with Langworthy Road (off to the left), which, in the early years of the century, did not pass across as far as Bolton Road — that extension came later. The tramcar is on its way from Eccles to Deansgate, Manchester. The early motor car, BA 210, belonged to Dr. Alexander Stewart, of Holly Bank, Eccles Old Road, and is parked outside his house, with the chauffeur standing by. The car was first registered in the motor taxation department on the 19th March 1906, and is listed as being a 'Horbick' tonneau of 10-12 horse power. 'Horbick' was the trade name of Horsfall & Bickham, of Bridgewater Works, Orchard Street, Pendleton, established 1835, a company mainly concerned with the textile trade, but which in 1904, due to the inventive nature of one of its managers, became one of the first firms in the region to manufacture motor vehicles. Its last car was produced in 1911. Dr.Stewart evidently believed in supporting local industry.

LONG WALK. SEEDLEY PARK.

Public parks offered many opportunities for the early postcard photographers, and general scenes and sporting activities made good subjects. Buile Hill Park was opened to the public in 1903. The mansion, now the Museum of Mining, was originally the home of Sir Thomas Potter, first Mayor of Manchester. Prior to the 1939-45 War, all Salford parks boasted a lake, most of which were inexplicably filled-in later. In this 1904 view the edge of the Buile Hill Park lake can be seen, together with the inevitable drinking fountain, well-patronised by the children, and the shelter, oddly-named a "summer shed."

Photographers were careful to distinguish between Buile Hill Park, which was the higher portion near Eccles Old Road, and Seedley Park, lower down the hill and close to Lower Seedley Road. Here is a view of the Long Walk, Seedley Park, looking towards Langworthy Road. Here, too, was a drinking fountain, seen in the middle of the picture. Local residents appear to be out for a Sunday afternoon stroll. The gentleman nearest the camera is sporting a shiny top hat, whilst the others wear bowlers. How long must it be since anyone went for a walk in a Salford park wearing a top hat?

As the number casualties mounted during the Great War of 1914-18, many cities found that their large public buildings, such as schools, were taken over to accommodate less-seriously wounded soldiers for whom there was no space in the proper hospitals. Such was the case in 1916, when Langworthy Road School (built 1898-99) was adapted to be a Military Hospital. Photographers produced postcards of both the exteriors and interiors of the buildings, so that inmates could send pictures of their temporary residence to their families. Here is a picture of a Religious Service being held in the main assembly hall of Langworthy Road School. Members of the nursing and medical staff are lined up at the rear of the hall. The soldier who sent this card to his wife in Scotland wrote, ''Here is a picture of our happy little home where we are all looked after so well. Why don't you write?''

An early postcard of the outside of the Langworthy Hotel on Langworthy Road shows that externally it has not changed very much. But regular patrons might be surprised to see this interior view, produced in 1902 by F.H.Walton of the Langworthy Road Post Office.

INTERIOR, LANGWORTHY HOTEL.   F. H. WALTON, Langworthy Post Office, Seedley.

The Sunday School Whit Walks were another favourite subject for photographers, who hoped to sell cards to those pictured taking part in the various processions. This example shows part of the Victoria Mission Church procession on Eccles New Road, Weaste, in 1909. The band is passing the Temperance Billiard Hall, which was situated near to the junction with Weaste Road. The sender of the card noted that the procession was headed by the Weaste Prize Band, with George Smith leading. The dignified and haughty George Smith may not have been amused at the group of small boys keeping in step alongside, nor at the trio standing in the roadway about to block the band's progress, one of whom seems to be more interested in the cameraman than the music. The driver of the tramcar waits patiently for an opportunity to overtake the musicians.

Tootal Road School (opened 1903, closed 1968) was another building taken over as a Military Hospital in 1916. Here some of the patients sun themselves in the school playground. Note the sign on the end of the building. The sender wrote, ''Well, Nellie, they have sent me back to hospital again, to my sorrow. Write to me at the 2nd General Hospital, Tootal Road, Weaste.'' Other wounded soldiers were accommodated in Fairhope House, Eccles Old Road, and in certain wards at Hope Hospital.

Hope Hospital was opened first in 1882 as the Salford Union Infirmary, or Workhouse. This postcard, from the 'Kingsway' series published by W.H.Smith, was sent in 1905 by a newly-arrived nursing sister to her parents in London, on which she wrote that ''The men working in the fields are all inmates.'' On close inspection, however, it looks rather as if the men are engaged in a cricket match. This is the side of the hospital which faced towards the railway and Eccles New Road, the tower to the right being one of the main entrances near Stott Lane. The tower was damaged during the 1939-45 War, and was dismantled, but the other buildings remain in use, though now hidden by modern extensions.

(HALF EDGE LANE, ECCLES (WINTER) 1906.

A photograph taken in December 1906 proves that the postcard publishers (in this case W. Whittaker of Irlams O' Th' Height) did occasionally brave the elements to capture a picturesque scene. The location is the junction of Eccles Old Road and Half Edge Lane, and the building centre left, which still survives, was the lodge at the entrance to Preston Avenue, at that time bearing a 'TO LET' sign. Notice that, although most of the roadway is impassable, snowploughs have cleared the tram tracks, and a lady is taking advantage of the cleared portion of Half Edge Lane. The gentleman in the bowler hat is presumably waiting for a tram, as the 'STOP' sign is on the nearby pole. The publisher's chosen title for the card is "Half Edge Lane, Eccles (Winter)." The word in brackets seems rather unnecessary! The sender has added the year in ink.

VICTORIA CRESCENT, ECCLES.

Numerous views were published during the Edwardian era of the various roads in Ellesmere Park, probably on the correct assumption that the people who lived in the large houses there would be avid writers of postcards. Victoria Crescent, lying roughly parallel to Half Edge Lane, and seen here in another 'Grosvenor Series' card, was the subject of at least four different views along its length. The boy carrying a basket on the right seems to be approaching a mobile greengrocery cart, and the view includes two other horse-drawn wagons, plus a hand cart. Further evidence of the amount of horse-drawn traffic may be noted on the surface of the roadway. Although parts of Ellesmere Park have changed but little over the century, a similar photograph today would include evidence of the motor car, rather than the horse.

A short walk along Gilda Brook Road from the old Eccles boundary near Half Edge Lane, would have brought one to Eccles Bridge. This early card by Harry Grundy was taken in 1903-4 from a spot in front of the station, and looks across towards the Congregational Church at the corner of Clarendon Road (behind the tramcar). The tramcar has halted at the entrance to Wellington Road. Gilda Brook Road is to the right. Note the newspaper seller positioned outside the station entrance — his mobile stand bears advertisements for the 'Manchester Guardian,' the 'Manchester Evening News,' the 'Daily Dispatch,' and the 'Weekly Times.' Across the road a long-skirted lady attired in black carries a parasol, whilst the gentleman beyond can only manage an ordinary umbrella on what must have been a very hot day. The horse and cart appear to be engaged in a household removal. The M602 motorway construction has ensured that nothing now remains of this scene, and one cannot now walk across the station bridge at this particular spot.

To the right of the photographer of the previous picture was the timber building which formed the entrance hall and booking office leading to the station platforms below the road. Eccles Station was a halt on the original 1830 Liverpool & Manchester Railway, later absorbed by the London & North Western Railway Company. The latter company constructed this building in 1881-82, when in response to the popularity of railway travel, and following the opening of the lines through Monton, Roe Green, and Worsley, the number of tracks between Cross Lane and Eccles was increased to four. On either side of the station entrance and incorporated in the building were small shops, one side occupied by Coop & Sons, Funeral Directors, and a confectioner, whilst to the right were Mr. Barber, 'High Class Tailor,' and the Station Cigar Stores. The tramcar on the left, on its route to Peel Green, has been fitted with an experimental top-cover — the crew pose obligingly for the photographer. This animated scene was captured in 1904 by Percy Greenhalgh of Weaste. The station buildings remained much the same until destroyed by fire in 1971. The ticket illustrated dates from L.M.S.R. days, when a child could travel from Eccles to Monton Green for one penny. Now, although the station remains open, only a tiny booking office appears at road level.

Eccles Cross was always regarded as the focal point and centre of Eccles life, and as such was the subject of numerous postcards throughout the Edwardian era. This Harry Grundy view of 1902-03, looking up Church Street, includes the remains of the old cross on the right, whilst its replacement, complete with drinking fountain, is in the centre of the picture. The horse trough alongside, looking rather like a large bath, is supported on six feet shaped like horses' hooves. Some of the buildings on the right remain today — the small building, which once housed at one and the same time, a hairdresser, cobbler, and an enamelling business, is now a health food shop. Next to it is the 'Hare & Hounds' Hotel, then under the control of the Irwell Street brewery of Watson, Woodhead & Wagstaffe, and across Fox Street is the Groves & Whitnall's establishment, the 'Fox Vaults.' On the extreme left is one of the oldest buildings in Eccles, sometimes called the 'Old Thatche,' claimed to have been built in 1094, and which sold Eccles cakes (made by Bradburn's, further up Church Street), herb beer, tobacco, confectionery, and ice cream (at 1d or ½d per glass). On the site of this shop was later built the new premises of Williams Deacon's bank in 1915. Notice that the large gas lamp standard has also been used as a signpost, one arm pointing to Patricroft, the other to Salford & Manchester. On the cart is a large wooden crate bearing the intriguing legend "Macdonalds Teeth Guaranteed." The remains of the old cross are the subject of separate postcards, some titled 'The Old Shrine,' others 'The Bull Baiting Stone,' but it is doubtful whether these descriptions were correct.

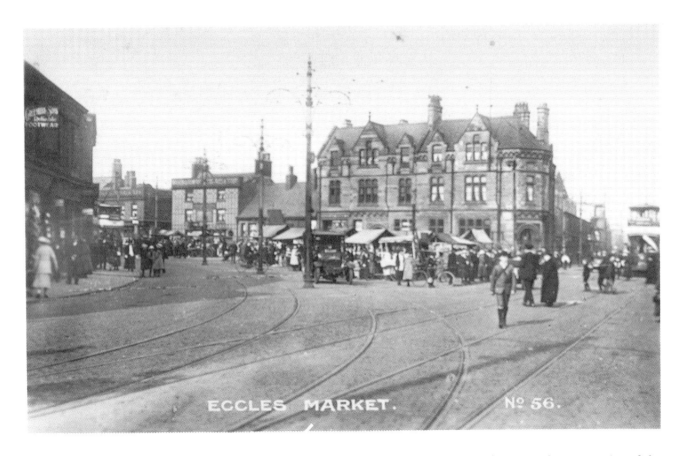

ECCLES MARKET. No 56.

A later picture of Eccles centre, by Charles Wilkinson, probably taken on a Saturday afternoon, shows a section of the busy street market, whose stalls used to spill out over the third and lesser-used side of the triangle of tram track near the bank on market days. The large building beyond the market stalls, originally the Manchester & County Bank, still serves the same function as a branch of the National Westminster network. It may be noted that the 'Hare & Hounds' public house has moved under the control of Walker & Homfray. The difference in fashions and the presence of a motor vehicle demonstrate that this was a scene from about 1921. The section of Church Street to the left is now closed to vehicles and 'pedestrianised,' and a large traffic island occupies the space in the foreground.

An example of a postcard which was never intended to be sent through the post is this advertisement card for the Eccles Picture Theatre Limited. On the reverse side were listed the programmes for the week, Monday to Wednesday offering a different selection of silent films from the Thursday to Saturday presentations. This would have been a give-away card, thrust into hands on the streets, or delivered through doors to entice local people to patronise the cinema. Prices were 6d, 1s, and 1s.6d, with no extra charge for reserving seats. All programmes were claimed to be ''Educational, Instructive, Amusing, and the most up-to-date pictures shown in Eccles.'' The Eccles Picture Theatre opened on the 28th June 1912, later becoming the 'Empire Picture Palace.' The building still exists as a carpet salesroom, opposite the end of Peel Street, on the corner of Corporation Road and Church Street.

Postcards produced by Eccles photographer Harry Grundy may be recognised by his initials 'HG' and a serial number at the bottom right-hand side of the print. Here, a view of Wellington Road, Eccles, posted in 1908, shows an absence of road traffic, save for the man riding the horse. Albert Road crosses in the foreground, with the old Liberal Club on the right. In the distance may be seen the spire of the Congregational Church at the corner of Clarendon Road, then that of the Wesleyan Chapel on the left, next to which was a third religious establishment, the 'New Connexion,' or 'Zion Methodist' Chapel, the site of which is now occupied by the new Liberal Club. This section of Wellington Road at one time boasted four religious premises, for the Eccles & Patricroft Railway Mission was also based here. Some buildings were demolished in the 1960s, and the right-hand side was much altered by the construction of the M602 motorway. Only the corner house on the left, once occupied by a local doctor, now remains.

Monton Green, traditionally an area of common land, was viewed about 1904-05 from the railway bridge over Canal Bank, again by photographer Harry Grundy, probably taking advantage of a sunny summer Sunday afternoon. An advertisement board for the Walker & Homfray's 'Blue Bell' Inn appears bottom right, whilst the inn itself (later re-named 'The Monton Green' but now reverted to 'The Blue Bell') appears centre top, towards Rocky Lane. The well-worn patch of land in the centre was later laid out as a public garden. The road leading over the canal and into Parrin Lane is on the left.

MONTON GREEN STATION.

London & North Western Ry
Issued subject to the conditions & regulations in
the Co.s Time Tables Books Bills & Notices & unless
stated therein to be as NOT available by Irish Mail.
MONTON GREEN TO
ECCLES
(K)
THIRD
CLASS   927(S)   [Parly
ECCLES   FARE ~ 1

98.II.24 x

Monton Green railway station, high above the road on an embankment, was opened by the London & North Western Railway Company in 1887, an intermediate stop on their Eccles to Wigan and Bolton lines. It preceded the spread of the electric tramways, and catered for the growing number of residents in this suburb. This photograph was taken from the Canal Bank side, and shows the steep enclosed stairway by which passengers had to reach the platforms. The spire of Monton Unitarian Church, on Monton Green, may be seen beyond the station. The ticket illustrated was used in 1896, when it was possible to travel from Monton Green to Eccles (Third Class) on the 'Parliamentary,' or workmen's train, for only one penny. When the electric tramways came a few years later, they rivalled the railways for local journeys, the cost of tramway travel being an average of 0.59d per mile. Monton Green Station closed in 1969, after which the bridges over Canal Bank and Parrin Lane were demolished, and the former track-bed in the direction of Worsley and Roe Green was turned into a pedestrian walkway. At the time of writing, there is a suggestion that the former course of the railway could be turned into a route for a future 'Metrolink' tramway line, but the destruction of a large section of the old route by the M602 motorway, plus the Lyntown Industrial Estate development, would necessitate the compulsory purchase of land and buildings. Considered alongside the construction of new bridgework which would now be necessary, this possibility seems rather unlikely.

The Bridgewater Canal from Worsley takes a sudden change of course at Monton, the result of a 1759 decision, after construction of the waterway had begun, not to cut the canal directly into Salford, which had been the original intention, but instead to cross the River Irwell at Barton and utilise a more southerly route to reach Castlefield, Manchester. Hence, the almost right-angled turn hard by Monton Bridge. The original canal bridge at Monton gave good service for many years, but when the electric tramway reached Monton in 1903, the old bridge was deemed to be unsuitable for any further extension of the system. Salford Corporation refused to proceed with lines to Winton and Worsley until Eccles Council had undertaken to reconstruct the bridge in a manner fit for the heavier vehicles. This postcard of the old bridge dates from about 1902-03, and shows the barge 'Annie' of Runcorn, operated by Simpson & Sons, passing beneath in the direction of Worsley. The barge would have been pulled by a horse, hidden from view on the towpath beyond. The house partly hidden by the bridge still exists. It was formerly the Lodge at the entrance to the Carriage Drive.

After some wrangling, Eccles Council awarded a contract for the new bridge at Monton to Messrs. Tate & Gordon, of Cheetham Hill Road, Manchester, and during 1904 Salford Corporation commenced construction of tramway lines in Parrin Lane and beyond, ready for the extension of services. The new bridge was completed in 1905. It was of strong girder construction, dwarfing the lodge building even more than the earlier structure. A more gentle gradient replaced the former hump-back. This view was taken from the sharp bend in the canal, looking along the straight to Worsley. The canal-side off-licence shop on the left offers ''Good Stabling, Hay, Oats, and Provender,'' as well as general stores and liquor for the boatmen. At this date, it was run by Mrs. Mary Agnes Browser, the business remaining in her family for many years afterwards. The building survives to this day as 'The Bargee' Inn and Restaurant, and the 1905 bridge carries heavy traffic daily as the sole connection between Monton and Winton. The other nearest bridges over the canal are at Patricroft in one direction, or Worsley in the other.

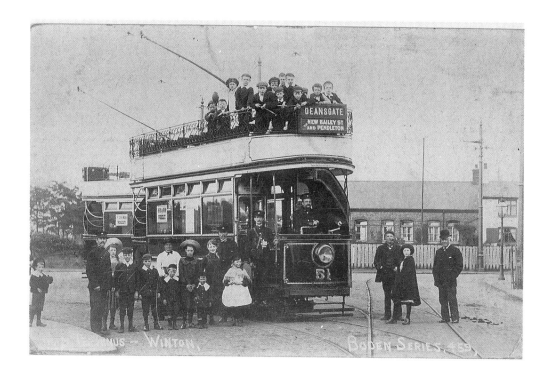

With the provision of the new bridge at Monton, the electric tramway could reach Winton and Worsley, and offered a second route to Peel Green via New Lane. Tram services to Winton commenced on the 1st June 1905, and William Boden, chemist, of Worsley Road, Winton, was on hand to record the scene. The junction at the end of Parrin Lane was peculiar in that the single-track from the Monton direction doubled at the junction and had two curves towards Peel Green, but only one in the Worsley direction. Here, two open-top tramcars are seen on the double curve, with an attendant crowd of onlookers, all anxious to get into the picture. Note the crowd of children on the top-deck — presumably not fare-paying passengers. As this is the first day of the new service, the regular crew members are joined by two tramway inspectors, there to see that all goes well. Although the new tramway track was complete as far as Worsley Court House, until 1912 passengers for Worsley had to dismount at this point and continue on foot, because Salford Corporation was reluctant to run what was thought would be an unprofitable service along Worsley Road. The cards hanging in the lower saloon windows of the tramcars therefore read "Monton & Winton, *for* Worsley." Long after the provision of covered-top tram-cars elsewhere on the system, Monton, Winton and Worsley residents had to bear with open-top cars because of the low railway bridges at Monton. In this view, premises of the old 'Brown Cow' Hotel may be noted on the right, a location now ruined and overshadowed by the outsize retaining wall and bridge of the motorway.

On the western side of Worsley Road, between Winton and the former boundary at Alder Forest, lies Albert Terrace (near Blantyre Street), a row of cottages built in 1866. This postcard, dated the 6th June 1909, shows the terrace as decorated for a Royal Visit. King Edward VII and Queen Alexandra passed by on the way to Worsley New Hall, where a troop review was held in the grounds, and local residents indulged in suitable celebrations. The terrace is still intact and recognisable, though the railings surrounding an excavation in the right foreground have long since gone.

An unusual card, not meant to be sent through the post, is this production by Baylis of Eccles, showing two floors of the Eccles Spinning & Manufacturing Company Limited, namely the Ring Spinning department and the Card Room. The mill was situated on Worsley Road, Patricroft, and the commemorative card was commissioned on the occasion of the 'Naming Of Engines' ceremony on the 11th May 1907. On the reverse side is printed the programme for the afternoon's event, which included music by Mr.T.Irving's band, refreshments, and an inspection of the mill, all of which culminated in the inauguration of the new steam engines which powered the factory. The naming was performed by the Mayoress of Eccles, Mrs. Schofield, and the toast to the success of the Company was proposed by Sir William Bailey, a noted Salford industrialist and director of the Trafford Park Industrial Estate.

Another Grundy view, this time of the junction of Worsley Road and New Lane, Winton, dates from about 1906-07. The sender has marked her house with a cross for the benefit of her mother, to whom the card was addressed. Other views of this spot sometimes call it 'The Market Place, Winton.' The row of shops exists today in slightly altered form. Note the signpost, pointing the direction of Peel Green and Warrington to the left, and Patricroft and Manchester to the right. The presence of one of Salford's single-deck tramcars, of which there were only ten, is unusual for this route. Because of their long wheelbase, the single-deck cars tended to de-rail easily on tight curves, and were therefore restricted in use. An exasperated tramways department first tried to sell them in 1907, but failing to find a buyer, they were eventually dismantled and their electrical equipment re-used in new vehicles by 1913.

An animated view of Liverpool Road, east of Green Lane, looking towards Eccles centre, shows one of the large double-deck bogie tramcars on the long route from Peel Green to Whitefield, via Manchester, which began late in 1903. The well-stocked shops on the left include Pool's Grocery Store; Watson's Boot Market, with strings of boots and shoes hung up outside on display; and J. Hurst's Pork Butcher's. The public house on the corner of Ellesmere Street may be glimpsed to the right. Once again, a gathering of children watch the photographer with interest.

Before the construction of the Manchester Ship Canal, small craft had been able to reach the quays of the city since 1734 by way of the Mersey and Irwell Navigation scheme, which had deepened the rivers, made a towpath, and constructed locks to ensure a good depth of water in each section of the course. One such lock was at Barton, not on the site of the present locks, but close to the Bridgewater Canal aqueduct, on the up-river, Eccles side of the waterway. This picture of the old locks at Barton is taken looking down-river, and includes part of the lock-keeper's house. Brindley's 1761 Bridgewater Canal aqueduct is seen passing across the centre of the picture. The competition from that undertaking forced the Mersey & Irwell Company to lower tolls and to oppose the Duke's scheme for an extension of his canal to Liverpool. Nevertheless, the Company continued to attract inward cargoes of cotton, timber and grain until about 1887. The old lock gates were removed during the construction of the Ship Canal in March 1891, but this postcard was not printed until about 1902. The publisher, Harry Grundy, titles his card the '*Old* Locks, Barton.' Part of the old road bridge can be glimpsed through the arch.

The Manchester Ship Canal opened for traffic in 1894, the work of construction having included new larger locks, deeper excavations and the straightening-out of several meanders. The Bridgewater Navigation Company, which by then held the rights of the Mersey & Irwell Company, had been purchased in 1887. Brindley's stone structure had to be replaced, and a new swing aqueduct (basically a sealed tank of water) was devised and constructed a short distance upstream from the original, so that traffic on the earlier canal would not be interrupted. Road bridges were also made to swing to permit the passage of large ocean-going ships. The new bridges at Barton proved a great attraction for the postcard photographers. This view shows the Bridgewater Canal aqueduct, and the road bridge beyond, swung open as a cargo liner is towed through in the direction of Salford Docks. The control tower lies between the bridges. The ship is the 'Manchester Trader,' displaying an alarming list to port as a Ship Canal Company tug takes the strain on the bow cable. The 'Manchester Trader,' the first of three ships to bear that name, was one of two vessels purchased by Manchester Liners Limited from the Elder Dempster Line in 1898 when the Company was founded specifically to trade from Manchester to North American ports. Her original name had been the 'Parkmore,' and as such she had been the first ship to bring Canadian grain in bulk to the new elevator on Trafford Wharf. She continued in the service of Manchester Liners until sold and renamed by new owners in 1913. Her eventual fate was to be torpedoed in the Mediterranean Sea in 1916.

S.S. "MANCHESTER TRADER" PASSING BARTON AQUEDUCT   COPYRIGHT

At crossing points on the canal where it was not worthwhile to build a bridge, ferries were provided, usually operated by boatmen for a small fee. 'Bob's Ferry' at Bob's Lane, Cadishead was merely a rowing boat, but the Irlam ferry, seen here, was somewhat more substantial. It was pulled across by the operator on the raised platform winding a cable, and its original purpose is revealed by the official title on the side, 'M.S.C. No.1 Horse Ferry.' In this example, a 1920s postcard, its cargo is a motor vehicle. The sender's message reads, "Dear Chum, I hope this picture won't give you the same problem as last time you saw it," leading one to speculate what the problem could have been!

Some postcards were produced to illustrate various leisure activities. In this case, the notice board of the C.W.S. Soap & Candle Works, Irlam, announces that the Social Club's Amateur Theatricals include the *second* performance of a farce entitled "Freezing A Mother-In-Law," also A Grand Concert Programme, with Dancing After 10.00 p.m. The postcard presumably shows the cast of the farce, which despite the costumes, appears to be an all-male affair. The gentleman standing in the centre sports a particularly unconvincing wig!

Cadishead lies on the main Manchester to Warrington road beyond Irlam, and is something of an outpost of the present Salford area. This fine view of a section of Liverpool Road, looking towards Eccles, shows the two railway bridges, the first of which clearly advertises its owning company as it marks the location of Cadishead's 'Cheshire Lines Station,' on the branch from Glazebrook Junction to Partington, Timperley, Cheadle, and Stockport. The lower bridge beyond carried the original track in 1873, but a deviation became necessary twenty years later to elevate the line to the required height over the Manchester Ship Canal, after which that part of the original route passed into Canal Company ownership, serving the sidings of the steelworks and the coaling basin. The ticket illustrated is for a special half-day excursion to Southport. The station closed in 1964. The children once again appear to be in their Sunday best clothes. It was common for postcard photographs to be taken in summer, when days were bright and when household fires did not contribute to the pollution of the atmosphere, and most likely on Sundays, when the air was clear of smoke from factory chimneys.

NO. 6   SWINTON PARK (NO. 2)   J.T.B.

Swinton Park, lying across the boundary between the old Salford and Swinton, was once very much more extensive than it is now. Originally, it included the land which is now part of the golf course, the East Lancashire Road, and the Westwood Estate. It contained many farms, and numerous postcards have survived showing ponds, grazing cattle, horses, and pleasant walks. This example, published by W.Lingard of Station Road, Swinton, shows one of the farmsteads, complete with ducks on the pond.

The 'Park Farm' had its own dairy at Irlams O' Th' Height, on the spot where now is found the car park for the Co-Op 'Shopping Giant' supermarket. Here is William Dunn Wibberley, dairyman, of 395 Bolton Road, the proprietor between 1909 and 1914, at the head of his 'milk float,' which contains his young assistant. Notice the window, which announces that ''new milk'' is delivered twice daily. Next door, number 393 at the corner of Brazil Street, is occupied by Harry Goodwin, Shoe Repairer, who evidently believed in the power of advertising. His shop front is adorned with a variety of slogans, including ''Profits Reduced To Shades Of Shadows,'' ''The Finest Possible Value That Brains, Capital And Enterprise Can Produce,'' and ''All Our Work Is Done Well, Looks Well, And Wears Well.'' Notice the prices advertised on the window, which indicate that the gentlemen paid one shilling more for their repairs than the ladies. Did the men have bigger feet?

Irlams O' Th' Height, at the division of the roads to Swinton and Pendlebury, lies at the former boundary of Salford. In this 1904 view, the camera was pointing up the Bolton Road, towards Pendlebury, with St. John's Church clock tower visible on the right. The tramcar, with one of the early top-covers, is headed for Pendlebury, to return via Station Road and Swinton. To the left of the tramcar is the old 'Britannia Inn.' The lady crossing the road wears a typical Lancashire shawl and apron, and in front of the inn is a family with a child in a 'bassinette,' or perambulator. The pole adorned with several gas lamps in the middle of the road, supports a gentleman who is watching the world go by, and is also home for three direction signs, that for the Swinton road being labelled for Chorley and Leigh. The East Lancashire Road was not constructed until 1933. Apart from St.John's Church, other buildings have been swept away in road improvement schemes.

DINNER TIME   WHEATSHEAF COLLIERIES

Which is you amongst this lot, G.A.

Postcards of the industrial scene are not so common, probably because, being less photogenic, the subjects were not likely to sell as well as the more general scenes. With the recent (1991) closure of Agecroft colliery, there are now no coal pits in the area, but this view from 1905 reminds us that the region was once an important centre of the mining industry. The card depicts 'Dinner Time' at the Wheatsheaf Collieries. The sender has written on the front of the card, ''Which is you amongst this lot?'' In the days before pit-head baths, miners had to return home unwashed. The two boys on the right may have been waiting for their father. The Wheatsheaf Colliery began production in 1846 and closed in 1961. The site, bounded by City Walk and Carrington Street, is now covered by the Wheatsheaf Industrial Estate, and betrays no hint of its former use.

PENDLEBURY PICTURE PALACE.

A scene further along Bolton Road, Pendlebury, taken from outside the 'Windmill Hotel' at the corner of Station Road, includes Winnard's 'Soda Fountain & Temperance Bar, next to a pawnbroker's shop, whose sign is not quite complete — it appears to have lost one of its three globes. On the other side of the alleyway is an 'off-licence' retailing ales and stout produced by the Worsley Brewery Company. The large building is the 'Pendlebury Picture Palace,' opened in 1912 for the showing of silent films. It now survives as a bingo hall, but the other buildings have gone. In the foreground, the tramway rails are curving into Station Road, off the picture to the right.

Another give-away advertisement card is this example from the Pendlebury Picture Palace. The interior of the cinema is shown on the front of the card, whilst the reverse carries details of the week's programme. On this occasion, the film being shown was "From Manger To Cross," described as "Kalem's Great Masterpiece," a religious epic in five parts, twice nightly at 6.45 and 8.45 p.m. Prices were threepence, fourpence and sixpence, and the card noted "Sixpenny seats (numbered and reserved) now booking in advance. No extra charge."

CLIFTON JN STATION.

Clifton Junction Station opened in 1847. It lay on the 1838 Manchester to Bolton Railway, to which the East Lancashire Railway Company had constructed a viaduct across the Irwell Valley in 1845 to carry their line from Radcliffe and Bury. Both original companies became part of the Lancashire & Yorkshire Railway. A third line, for mineral traffic, was constructed by the London & North Western Railway in 1850. In this view, looking towards Manchester, the Bolton line is to the right, whilst centre left can be seen the platforms for the Bury branch. In the foreground, the mineral line from Patricroft passes beneath the Bolton tracks, forming the third side of the triangle as it rises to join the Bury line at Molyneux Junction, off to the left of the picture. Only the Bolton line platforms now remain, and the station is classed as an unstaffed halt. Traffic on the mineral line came to a premature end when the 'Black Harry' Tunnel beneath Temple Drive, Swinton, collapsed in 1953. Passenger trains were withdrawn on the Clifton to Bury section in December 1966, and the line was closed to all traffic in the following year. Afterwards the impressive viaduct which carried the line over the valley was demolished. The M62 motorway now crosses the valley floor in its place.

When the Lancashire & Yorkshire Railway wanted to compete with the London & North Western Company's line to Liverpool, a new route was opened in 1887, branching from the Bolton line near Windsor Bridge, and with new stations at Pendleton ('New,' or Broad Street), Irlams O' Th' Height, Pendlebury, Swinton, Moorside, and Walkden. Swinton Station entrance hall, on Station Road, was built above the tracks in the same yellow brick which characterised other stations on this line. Though Pendlebury Station closed in 1960, the Swinton building remains open and may be compared with the similar structure above the tracks at Moorside & Wardley, which is also still in use. In this 1904 view the old semaphore signals may be noted above the bridge to the right. On the left was formerly situated the railway goods yard. The peculiarly-shaped building on the corner of Cromwell Road, which is still to be seen, was then a refreshment room and shop occupied by Samuel Wolstenholme, confectioner. The small boy in the middle of the road seems oblivious to the danger from the approaching tramcar.

The Swinton Church end of Station Road shows a Salford tramcar approaching the junction with Chorley Road about 1920. In the foreground, tracks of the South Lancashire Tramways system curve from Partington Lane. Though both tramway companies were anxious to complete the junction at this point, intransigence on the part of the Swinton Council prevented progress, and the tracks were not connected until 1926, when after only one day of operation of a through route from Manchester to Walkden, the service came to a temporary halt because of the General Strike. The corner shop to the right was that of chemist Ebenezer Yates. Today, we would be looking at the Lancastrian Hall. On the opposite corner, the Bull's Head Hotel, formerly in the Worsley Brewery chain, remains.

26 STATION ROAD, SWINTON

Further along Chorley Road, in the direction of Swinton Market Place, was the old Swinton Post Office, later replaced by a new building on the opposite side of the road. In this 1920s view, the old Post Office lies between Kenyon's Tailoring and Wilkinson's Shoe Shop, still trading on the same spot, but at that date sporting a verandah. This particular row of shops remains today, but those beyond were demolished for the construction of the shopping precinct in the 1960s. In the distance may be seen a smoking mill chimney, and on the left the wall surrounding the Industrial Schools.

The land occupied by the Swinton Town Hall (built 1936-37 and since 1974 home to the Salford Civic Centre), was formerly the site of the Swinton Industrial Schools, which lay at right angles to Chorley Road, parallel to Partington Lane. The schools had been founded in 1843 by the Manchester Poor Law Guardians as an alternative to the workhouse, and were intended to provide a home and training for poor children. They were described by Charles Dickens on a visit in 1850 as "a pauper palace." The schools were closed in 1925, but the buildings were not demolished until 1933.

This view of Worsley Road, Swinton, as seen from the end of Partington Lane, may seem familiar because the Methodist Free Church building (now the Worsley Road Methodist Church) is still to be seen. However, the rest of the scene is vastly different. In 1933 the highway was bisected by the then new East Lancashire Road, opened 'officially' in 1934 by King George V and Queen Mary, who travelled along it after visiting the Mersey Tunnel. Today a similar viewpoint would include the crossroads and traffic signals of a very busy junction.

The reverse side of this postcard is worth study as a reminder of the reliability and speed of local postal deliveries. The halfpenny Edward VII stamp has been cancelled at 9.15 a.m. on October 27th 1903. The young lady who wrote ''Just a reminder that I won't be home to tea tonight,'' and addressed the card to Miss Currie, Hazelhurst, Swinton, could post it the same morning, and be absolutely confident that the addressee would receive it by the mid-day delivery.

Brunswick Chapel, Broad Street. *1903* Pendleton.

FOLLY LANE, SWINTON W.D. No.23

The junction of Dales Brow (left) and Folly Lane has a deserted air in this postcard. The children lend some interest to the scene. On the left, a boy adjusts the wheel of his hand-drawn fuel cart, whilst amongst the group in the centre is a young boy in a toy pedal car. Unusually, this spot is immediately recognisable today.

The Swinton & District Steam Laundry had premises on Worsley Road, between Shaftesbury Road and Lyon Street. In the days of domestic washing machines, we tend to forget how important was the regular collection and return of laundered and starched clothes. Here, the young men in charge of cart number 5 pause in their daily round as they pose for the cameraman.

Further along Worsley Road, and over the border into Worsley itself, was Worsley Station, opened 1864, the next stop along the London & North Western Railway Company's line from Monton Green. Here is seen the approach road sloping down to the station entrance, where a horse-drawn carriage awaits patrons from the next train. Worsley Station remained in use for just over a century, closing when the line was abandoned in 1969. The approach road is still recognisable opposite the end of Greenleach Lane, though lush and unchecked vegetation encroaches from the hedgerows. The station buildings and footbridge have gone, but the platform edges, though neglected and overgrown, are still visible from the pedestrian walkway.

Approaching Worsley Village along Worsley Road, the traveller would pass first The Green and then the original Post Office, opposite an old corn mill. Postmistress Mrs.Ford ran the telegraph office and the savings bank, as well as dealing with all other duties. This early postcard shows the Post Office on the left. The cameraman was looking in the direction of Worsley Court House, across the bridge which spanned the entrance to the underground canal system.

BOAT HOUSE WORSLEY

A favourite subject for both artists and photographers was the Worsley Packet House and bridge. This postcard is one of W.Whittaker's productions, and must date from before 1904. The corn mill, centre right in the picture and on the Delph side of the bridge, had been disused since about 1889, and was demolished by 1904 to make way for a new Post Office. Note the collection of 'starvationer' barges in the waterway leading to the entrance to the 53-or-more miles of underground canals, which were designed to allow mined coal to be transported direct from the pits on to the Bridgewater Canal at this point. Though coal ceased to be brought out this way in 1889, the underground canal network remained a valuable drainage system for the mines, and today the ochre leached from the rock gives the main canal its distinctive colouring at this point.

The demolition of the old corn mill gave space for the construction of a new Post Office near Worsley Delph. The new structure was built on the opposite side of the road from the original, and was given a half-timbered frontage, which made it look older than it really was. Between it and Mill Brow was ''Lady Ellesmere's Coffee Tavern,'' run by one Howell Augustus. In this 1906 postcard, the tar boiler and debris in front of the Post Office provide evidence of some road repairs, possibly connected with the South Lancashire Tramway system, which had just reached this spot from Atherton and Boothstown. The open-top tramcar on the right, destination Boothstown, has a placard hung over the dash plate which reads ''TAKE THIS CAR FOR WORSLEY & SWINTON.'' On the left, two young boys wait with their truck, which they are probably about to fill with coal for the household. Further on a man holding a milk pail watches the gentleman ride by. Today, the 1905 Post Office building is a restaurant and shops, the third Worsley Post Office being round the corner in converted premises on Barton Road.

WORSLEY.

The centre of Worsley Village is the road junction near to the Court House. In this view before the tramway days, the Court House is seen much as it is now, but the building on the right, the Grapes Hotel, an old eighteenth century coaching inn which stood opposite the end of Worsley Road, was demolished in 1902 to make way for a new entrance for Worsley New Hall. The Grapes was replaced by the Bridgewater Hotel, further along Barton Road.

The new gatehouse which was constructed in 1903 on the site of the old Grapes Hotel, stood at the entrance to one of the carriage drives leading to the New Hall. It boasted an impressive entrance arch, with coat-of-arms in the stonework. It also provided a second home for the famous clock from the Duke of Bridgewater's workshops on The Green. This clock had been specially adapted to strike thirteen at one o'clock, and was reported to have been the Duke's answer to tardy workmen who claimed they could not always hear the single chime which recalled them to their afternoon labours. At the side of the arch was the gatekeeper's lodge, at this period the home of Robert C. Gray, who cut a splendid figure in his uniformed livery. The arch and lodge outlived the destruction of the Hall, but the structure was dismantled in 1959, and the site is now occupied by a traffic island at one of the motorway access roads.

In this view of Worsley Village, Barton Road, photographed by William Boden about 1905, one of the lamps at the entrance to the Bridgewater Hotel forecourt may be seen behind the children on the left. The row of cottages is now much altered and adapted for shops, and includes the third Worsley Post Office in one of the converted cottages. The larger building beyond the terrace was once the Worsley 'Constabulary,' or Police Station. In the distance is St.Mark's Church. Once again, the costumes of the children suggest that it was probably a Sunday. Note the lady pushing the large-wheeled bassinette.

The canal at Worsley is seen here from the Boothstown side of the Barton Road bridge, looking towards 'Worsley Turn' by the Packet House. A string of three well-laden coal barges (nearest one 'Willie') glides along the canal in the direction of Manchester. The footpath climbing to the right, where the small boys wait by the railings, leads to the main road. The scene is not much altered today, except that the commercial traffic on the canal has been replaced by pleasure craft.

Leigh Road, Worsley, was once called Chaddock Road, not to be confused with the present Chaddock Lane at Boothstown. Certain parts of this road had to be adapted and widened to permit the construction of the tramway from Boothstown in 1906, but in this earlier view the bridge carrying the footpath connecting Worsley Old Hall (to the right) with the New Hall was still intact. Though the central portion of the bridge has gone, the abutments may still be seen on either side of Leigh Road. In the centre distance, to the right of the road, may be glimpsed the Monument erected in 1859 as a tribute to the first Earl of Ellesmere. Also on Leigh Road, just a few yards from the motorway exit, and not far from the aforementioned bridge abutments, may be seen another former entrance to the New Hall, complete with impressive wrought-iron gates, whose craftsmanship, when new, was admired sufficiently to be placed on display at a London exhibition.

Worsley New Hall was built for the Earl of Ellesmere in 1845. The south side, facing down to the canal and with an aspect across the Cheshire Plain, is seen here from across the ornamental lake. William Boden, the Winton photographer, produced a series of postcards of the Hall and its gardens about 1907, and most other local photographers seem to have published views of the buildings, its famous visitors, or the events held in its grounds in the early years of the century. More postcards from the 1916-18 period show it in use as a temporary Military Hospital for wounded soldiers, when nursing staff (and concert party members to entertain the inmates) were granted free travel on the tramcars to and from Worsley. It was used again in the Second World War by American servicemen on experimental duties, but, sadly, was demolished in 1949. The lake may still be seen as part of the Middlewood Scout Camp, and the Worsley Hall Garden Centre occupies a portion of the grounds. At the Garden Centre, traces of the former layout of the Hall's kitchen gardens may be observed, and the Gardener's Cottage survives.

In 1851 the Earl of Ellesmere had a vessel built so that Queen Victoria and Prince Albert could be met on arrival at Patricroft Station and enjoy the pleasure of sailing to Worsley New Hall on the canal, disembarking at a specially-constructed landing stage. The vessel became known as 'The Royal Barge,' sometimes 'The State Barge,' and was, indeed, used by royalty on a number of subsequent occasions. The barge was drawn along by two grey horses, ridden by smartly-attired postillions, and was used many times for visitors to the Egerton family home. It was 45 feet long, painted white with red and gold lining, and had a handsome cabin in the best Victorian style, carved bow, armorial bearings, cherubs, and other ornamentations, and a tiller carved in the shape of a serpent. The barge was usually moored in the boathouse by Worsley Green. In this postcard of June 1914, the passengers are local people costumed for taking part in the Worsley Historical Pageant, held in the Hall grounds. The vessel subsequently passed into the possession of the Manchester Ship Canal Company, and was named 'Earl Of Ellesmere.' In 1931 modifications were carried out to make the barge suitable for conveying parties around the Docks. A motor was fitted, and, in view of the vessel's historical importance, nine carved figures, the figure head and the tiller were removed for safe keeping. By 1937 the barge was said by the Harbour Master to be in a 'delapidated state,' of no use to the Company, and an 'unnecessary commitment.' Tragically, in October 1938 the Royal Barge was sold to a Trafford Park timber merchant for £5. The fate of the carvings in 'safe keeping' is not known.

Some postcards were specially published to commemorate particular events or deeds. This W.H.Smith example, issued in 1906, was to celebrate the achievements and mark the birthplace of John Thomas Tyldesley, of Roe Green, a Lancashire County Cricket Club player between 1895 and 1916. At the start of the century he was considered to be the finest professional batsman in England. After the issue of this card, the achievements of J.T.Tyldesley were matched by his younger brother, Ernest, who, between 1909 and 1936 became the most prolific batsman in the history of the County, scoring 38,874 runs, including 102 centuries.

J.T. TYLDESLEY = LANCASHIRE. C.C.
and his birthplace, ROE GREEN, WORSLEY.

W.H.S. & S., M. Copyright. 1906.

Photo. P. G. Hunt.

WALKDEN STATION   HG 121

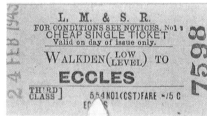

Along the London & North Western Company's railway from Worsley through Roe Green lay Walkden Station, opened 1875, on the line to Little Hulton and Bolton. This view, taken from Park Road bridge, includes several features still recognisable today — the Ellesmere Hotel on the left, at the corner of Walkden Road and Brindley Street; the shops at the corner of Birch Road; the former Town Hall of Worsley Urban District Council (opened 1911), and the Technical College, right. When the Lancashire & Yorkshire Railway Company's rival Walkden Station opened in 1888, only a few yards away at the junction of Memorial Road and Walkden Road, it became known as 'Walkden High Level,' whilst the L.N.W.R. was 'Low Level.' Both lines passed into the London, Midland & Scottish group in 1923. The ticket shown dates from 1943, when the fare from Walkden to Eccles was fivepence. The 'Low Level' station closed in 1954 with the abandonment of that length of line, but the High Level Station remains in use.

An example of a small street, with few houses, yet still considered worthy of the postcard photographer's attention, is this view of Wilfred Road, Walkden. All the buildings seen in the photograph still exist, but the later St.George's Crescent now leaves at the right of the picture. The photograph was taken looking towards and across Memorial Road. On the far side of Memorial Road is what appears to be a wheelwright's repair yard, and the premises of the former police station (with its small balcony) may be noted at the junction of Stanley Road and Memorial Road. The handcart, apparently abandoned in the middle of the road, is a basket-weave delivery cart. On the right, some young men obligingly wait motionless until the photographer's work is finished. Behind the cameraman would have been the headgear of Mangall's Colliery, on a site now occupied by the British Legion Club.

A view of Manchester Road, Walkden, with the photographer facing towards Swinton, includes the tower of St.Paul's Church on the left, and the horse trough and drinking fountain which once stood in the centre of the roadway opposite the Stocks Hotel. The drinking fountain was a gift from the Walkden Co-Operative Society to mark the coronation of King Edward VII in 1901. Once again, the inevitable collection of small boys watches the cameraman with interest.

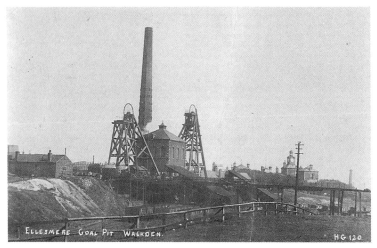

ELLESMERE COAL PIT WALKDEN.   HG 120

Evidence of Walkden's industrial past is provided by this 1905 postcard of the Ellesmere Coal Pit, which was situated close to Walkden centre. The pit ceased production in 1921, but the buildings and some underground equipment continued in use as a pumping station for the drainage of other mines in the district, the pumped water being discharged into the underground canal system, across which it lay. This activity ceased in the late 1960s, and the surface structures were demolished. Middle right, behind the telegraph pole, may be noted the tower of the Bridgewater Trustees' offices in Bridgewater Road. Walkden Yard workshops, for the maintenance and repair of the locomotives of the Manchester Collieries group, lay to the right, off Tynesbank.

Boothstown was originally a small village on the road between Leigh and Swinton. A view of Leigh Road about 1906 shows Walker & Homfray's 'Greyhound Hotel' on the right, innkeeper Timothy Jas. Oldfield, advertising its good stabling and bowling green. The group of children includes one young man who has been unable to keep still during the few seconds whilst the photographer's plate was being exposed.

The South Lancashire Tramways Company's line from Atherton reached Boothstown in 1905. For a while the tram terminus was at Stirrup Bridge, seen here looking up the slope towards Coupe Brow, Chaddock Lane branching off to the left in front of the chapel. The tram-tracks end abruptly where the children are standing in the middle of the road. Not until September 1906 was the service extended from this spot to Worsley and Swinton. This circuitous route eventually ran to Farnworth, and was converted to operation by trolley-buses from 1931 until 1958.

A rural scene in Vicars Hall Lane, Boothstown, about 1903, shows a young man resting his milk pail in a road empty save for his small friends, all of whom are sporting clogs.

Finally, another scene from the harsh winter of 1906-07, when Frederick Rogerson of Boothstown braved the weather to record the snowy conditions in which the driver of this coach (wearing his top hat) and his well-muffled passenger took to the road on the 28th December 1906 — frozen in time, one might say. The only F. Rogerson recorded in the old street directories of Boothstown for that period lived at 191 Leigh Road, and his occupation was listed as railway signalman. Perhaps postcard photography was a side-line.

SALFORD
LOCAL HISTORY LIBRARY

The Local History Library, situated in the city's Art Gallery and Museum at Peel Park, houses an extensive collection of items of local interest.

The collection includes photographs, newspapers, periodicals, maps, plans, posters, parish registers, census returns etc, etc.

If you are interested in the history of our city a visit to this library is a must.

OPENING HOURS: LIBRARY — 10am to 5pm Monday, Tuesday, Thursday, and Friday: 10am to 9pm Wednesday; Closed Saturday and Sunday.

ART GALLERY & MUSEUM — 10.00am to 4.45pm Monday to Friday; closed Saturday; 2.00pm to 5.00pm Sunday.

ADDRESS: Salford Local History Library, Peel Park, Salford M5 4WU.
Tel. 061-736 2649

STAFF: Tim Ashworth (Local History Librarian), Tony Frankland (Asst. Local History Librarian), Sandra Hayton (Library Assistant), Patricia Nuttall (Library Asst.).

Interested in local history? Why not join the Salford Local History Society, a friendly group formed to encourage and facilitate the study of all aspects of local history in the rapidly-changing City of Salford? Come along to one of our meetings and meet people with similar interests. We arrange lectures, discussions, slide shows, visits to places of historic interest, and issue a monthly newsletter to members. Meetings are held on the last Tuesday of every month (except December), commencing at 7.30p.m., in Midwood Hall, Eccles Old Road, Pendleton, Salford 6. Midwood Hall is situated close to the junction of Eccles Old Road and Bolton Road, and buses 64, 66, 67, 68 and 127 stop nearby.

THE
MANCHESTER MAN

by MRS. G. LINNÆUS BANKS

OUR BLITZ

RED SKIES OVER MANCHESTER
A WARTIME FACSIMILE

MANCHESTER
TRAMS & BUSES

Ted Gray

New enlarged edition

Also Available From 'MEMORIES'